Becoming A Trophy Husband: Divorce-Proof Your Marriage

GREGORY D. MOSTELLA, DMIN

Gregory D. Mostella

DEDICATION

To my Trophy Bride — Michelle. Thank you for believing in my ability to teach what I have learned, your gentle persistence, and your patience as I wrote and rewrote. To Trophy Wives, present and future, thank you for believing and investing in your marriage and your potential Trophy Husband. Although we men don't always purchase or read books we might need to read, we are more likely to read books you buy or recommend. I pray that your trophy husband loves you as you desire, and I pray the blessings of Proverbs 31:28 in your life – "May your husband wake up and your children, blessing and giving praise to God for you."

To Trophy Husbands and Trophy Dads, I applaud you for investing in yourself and your family. I set out in this writing to share some essential life lessons in print. These are lessons I wish I had known about as a young man. Many men feel they don't need help becoming men or learning from someone else's experience. But those who are wise know that we learn everything from someone else and that there is always more we can learn. If we can instill a fraction of these lessons in other men, they will make fewer mistakes that might derail them in life.

CONTENTS

THE PROVERBS 31 HUSBAND

He fully trusts his wife and does not fear losing her or their goods. He succeeds in life because she is at his side. (11-12)

He is well-known and sits among the city's leaders because she honors and promotes him. (23)

He awakens, leading the children in praising his wife and their mother. (28)

1 INTRODUCTION

Trophy Husbands are men whose wives boast about them to their family and friends. They honor and respect their wives, and they keep working to improve. The Trophy Husband LOVES his wife with the same tenacity and passion he hopes to receive.

He UNDERSTANDS that to win her heart; he must open his heart; He HONORS, ESTEEMS, and EMBRACES his spouse as his partner; He ACCEPTS her contributions as beneficial to their mutual success and is relentless in his devotion.

Michelle, my bride of 16 years, has told me for most of our marriage that I "should be teaching men to become great husbands." --Wow! – My wife thinks I can teach other men to be great husbands. Truthfully, I have never thought of myself as doing anything spectacular or different from other men. I love my wife and keep looking for ways to show it. I try to love her the way she needs to be loved. My bride is the best thing that ever happened to me, and I get pleasure from seeing her happy.

So that's it – that's what she has been seeing in me. I am blessed to have a partner who loves me in return and who believes in me. So, in honoring her belief in me, I have combined my first 26 lessons under this cover.

If you are married or want to marry, here is your initial and essential guide. Fathers and mothers will find it especially beneficial in teaching dating-age sons and daughters. Your sons will be more mindful of how they choose and treat their wives, and your daughters will be better informed and more selective in choosing a husband. Pastors, teachers, and counselors will also find these teachings indispensable in counseling and instruction.

I get it that some husbands feel they can never attain trophy status -- I know too many men who think their spouse has hardened to the point that there is no hope. I have counseled men and women who seem only to tolerate their marriages as if waiting for themselves or their partner to die. And with others who believed there was no hope their mate would ever again see them in a positive light. They live together like unhappy roommates. Yes, I get it – relationships are complicated, and marriages take hard work. But, if Lazarus could get up from the grave, so can your marriage. Anything is possible when one is willing to learn a few tools and work consistently.

Becoming the right kind of husband is a way of cheat-proofing your marriage and ensuring against divorce, in addition to other benefits.

If it looks like you are already heading for a breakup, this book is your best investment. Don't throw in the towel without reading "Becoming A Trophy Husband: Cheat-Proof Your Marriage."

2 APPRECIATE HER

When you marry, and your wife accepts your name; gives birth to your children; shares your home and life; she should know she is first on your mind when you wake up and the last on your mind when you lie down. Master appreciating your spouse; she will look forward to your coming home. She will make your home a joyful place to work, live and play. She will extend your life and your productivity and legacy.

Everyone needs to feel valued and appreciated by those they love—especially your bride. Demonstrating your appreciation for her will extend your honeymoon into a lifetime. Attending to and anticipating her needs and putting them before your own is a way of showing gratitude to your mate.

Become a Servant in Your Marriage

Becoming a servant does not mean being a stepstool, hen-pecked, or weak, but communicating to her that "Nothing is more important to me than you."

You become a servant by attentively listening to what she says and following up on your commitments. Whether it's something she mentions daily, like a cabinet door that needs adjusting, or something she only hints at once -- like, "I'd like us to go to church together." You get high marks for listening and responding if she has only said it once. If she repeatedly mentions something, you have some catching up to do.

Demonstrate Selfless Devotion

Demonstrating selfless devotion to your mate is the best example of sacrifice and committed love. You will be your wife's champion and your child's best example of how to marry well and value and be valued by a spouse. Your commitment will pay great dividends in your family for many generations.

3 BOOST HER

Occasionally, your mate might need you to lift or support her while she reaches for something overhead. I already know you will be up for that. But she will also require you to boost her confidence and esteem by recognizing her beauty, intellect, achievements, and abilities. Here are three keys for giving that support:

LISTEN TO HER - Fellows, the best advice I can offer in marriage is – L-I-S-T-E-N. We can't possibly see, know and do everything ourselves. Ask for, accept, and appreciate your wife's help. Didn't you marry because you couldn't live without her? Don't start trying to live without her in marriage.

As men, we are not always the best listeners. If you are the least like me, sometimes, a single word can trigger us to respond before we hear the complete statement. When your spouse tells you, "Something broke,"

you might find yourself rushing off to fix it before realizing she said she fixed the problem. Men have an inborn "fix-it" mentality that often keeps us from hearing. Your ability to hear your spouse is far more critical than being able to fix everything. More than half of the problems you will face in life will be rectified just by effective listening.

It takes effort, but hear her out completely. Whatever else you may be doing, put it aside when she wants to talk, and do your best to listen. You listening to her reminds her that she is important to you. It not only gives her a boost but raises your stock. Attending to what she says could be your most important role as a trophy husband.

ENCOURAGE HER - Your mate will significantly benefit from your encouragement, even if she is the most confident person you know. We all experience highs and lows in life, and we profit when others express hope and confidence in us.

SUPPORT HER. -Support your mate, even when you don't fully agree with her choices. If she is not planning to rob a bank, topple the government, or murder someone, stick with her like "sidewalk chewing gum." Support her morally, financially, emotionally, spiritually, romantically, and in any other way necessary. Your wife is not expecting you to be her. She wants to know that you are alive, love her, and that you are interested in and care about what she thinks and feels.

3 COMPLIMENT HER

Continue to speak well of your bride, no matter how long you have been married. She can know that she is beautiful and her dress is stunning, but it will not mean as much if you don't recognize and acknowledge it. Others may tell her how radiant her skin is, notice how great she looks, and take note of her new hairstyle, but nothing takes the place of the one she loves raving about it.

Speaking well of the woman you love in the dark or alone misses the mark. Your loved one should always know that you have her back. Never miss an opportunity to rave about her, whether alone or in the company of others. Take note — it works both ways, just as you stand a little taller when she tells others about you. Try it and watch her blush, then inch closer to you.

Your words can transform her mood and disposition. See something you like? Make a big deal about it without her asking. You should know that most women who have had extra-marital flings received attention from the outside they were not receiving in their marriage.

Rest assured that when you make all those beautiful deposits to your mate's self-esteem at home, she will quickly forget everything others say and rush home to you.

Make Your Marriage More Affairs Proof

1. Be sincere. You convey sincerity by looking into your mate's eyes through your touch, your voice, and the words you use.

2. Compliment her often, most of all when she seems discouraged or vulnerable.

3. Spend quality time with her, listening, reflecting, remembering, and making memories.

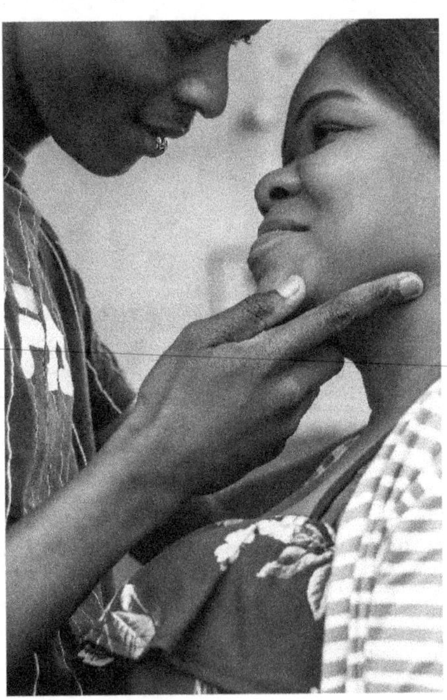

4 DREAM DATES

Dreams in and of themselves are already powerful, but multiplied by two, who knows what might be possible? Use your combined imagination to plan dates, trips, vacations, and home-building projects. What do you want to do; where do you want to go? Dreaming together brings you closer in all areas of your relationship.

As we indicated before, it is easy to fall into ruts in marriage, and day-to-day work routines can harm our relationships. Our schedules become more challenging once we add children. We must now contend with medical appointments, childcare, school events, etc.

If you and your spouse work outside the home, the strain on the marriage can become overwhelming and adversely impact the relationship because you no longer have enough time for each other. Act when these challenges arise. Discuss your dreams and use them to plan together so that life doesn't sneak up on you. Where would you like to be in five years? Is a bigger home in your future? Do you need financial planning? Talking about your dreams and nightmares now can ensure you have more leisure time together in the future.

Date to Celebrate

Don't just dream – CELEBRATE TOGETHER when your dreams become a reality. That magical time together is called DATING.

You must schedule time for dating. Initially, there may be very little time. But, as you commit to planning, organizing, and finding those you can trust to provide childcare, you will gradually feel comfortable leaving your children with others and begin to enjoy time with each other.

Start with a simple date every two to three weeks, dinner, a movie, or a social event in an intimate setting. A little trade secret for you guys - she will love that you planned the entire date while considering her considerations. Just tell her, "Honey, I want to take you out on such-and-such day and time; I am making the arrangements, including childcare and pet care. Please be ready at...."

Gradually, work toward an overnight and then a weekend stay. Use your imagination for planning. Married dates can be as simple as staying at a new hotel. The key is to get started, and remember you never get so old that this is not enjoyable. Even if you are a married senior, get back to dating! Don't forget to take along some fun stuff, like her favorite massage oils, lotions, your favorite sleepwear, and a copy of our book, **Seven Keys to Better Sex in Marriage, available at bit.ly/getthe7keys**

5 ENGAGE HER

In today's climate, it is relatively easy to become trapped in the routine of leaving home, going to work, coming home to sleep, going back to work, and repeating the cycle until the weekend. Life becomes routine, monotonous, and dull, wreaking havoc on family relationships. Take the time to enjoy life with those you love.

One of your key roles as a husband is to keep things moving in a positive direction that is enjoyable and engaging. Take time to have fun. Plan a movie night, picnic, backyard barbecue, and a beach or lake trip together. Then periodically plan a surprise outing for the two of you. Arrange for childcare without involving her by choosing a sitter she knows and trusts. When you work out the details, inform her on the way to your outing so that she can relax without worry.

Avoid being so busy earning a living that you are not living. Wealth means nothing if you cannot enjoy it with those you love. Practice engaging with your family. Telling amusing stories and jokes is a means of entertaining and a means of teaching your children. It will be one of the things they fondly remember about you for many years to come.

Ensure your family participates in family reunions, trips to recreational events, amusement parks, National parks, and museums. Families also benefit from theatrical presentations, like plays, ballet, and musicals. Consider taking regularly scheduled photos for your family album and loved ones who live in other cities. Use social media to connect with in-laws and 'outlaws.'

Don't wait for special occasions to celebrate. Look for ways to make magic. Learn to be spontaneous. Come up for air occasionally. Don't let making a living keep you from living to the fullest.

6 FIGHT FAIR & FORGIVE

Even in the best relationships, disagreements, and fallouts will happen. At our house, we call them "periods of intense fellowship." At some point, you will argue — whether it is about the preferred position of the toilet seat, money, chores, children, and friends -- there will be contention. I will let you in on a secret. If you are not working to improve, most of the time, it will be about something you said, did, or failed to do. So, buckle up and start upgrading your trophy status. When you work at it, arguments will be fewer, farther apart, and less of a blowout.

Three Rules for Fighting Fair:

1. **NEVER abuse your mate, verbally or physically.** I emphasize again that lighting should not become physical, even if she hits you first. You may laugh at the suggestion, but it happens. More and more, women are the aggressors.

If you are parenting, teach your daughters and sons to avoid risky situations to identify bullying and abuse, including cyberbullying. Teach them about setting boundaries,s and respecting other people's space.

Teach youngsters to use conflict resolution skills and show when walking away is appropriate. Beware of the increase in incidences of bullying and extorting sexual favors through blackmail, force, or group influence via social media. These acts are becoming more common among teens and preteens and are a factor in youth suicides. You owe it to your child to be more informed in these matters.

If you are dating, avoid dates that tend to be handsy, swatting and pushing others away without realizing they are doing so. I am not suggesting that such a person is abusive, but behaving this way might cause someone to feel they need to defend themselves.

2. **NEVER hit below the belt.** You know those things your loved one is sensitive about -- appearance, weight, speech, education level, and family. Avoid bringing anything up in a fight that she cannot help — even in jest. Avoid discussing anything she shared with you in confidence unless she mentions it. Using these topics in a dispute can cause wounds you might not realize for many years.

3. **NEVER raise any concern with put-downs, malice, and grudges.** In addressing grievances, remember that your loved one is not your enemy; you are on the same team. In the end, forgive, ask for forgiveness, then kiss, make up, and let it go.

Five Benefits of Fighting Fair:

1. Fighting Fair offers a chance to understand the problem.
2. It permits you to clarify your roles or positions.
3. It allows an opportunity for a fresh start.
4. It will enable forgiving and receiving forgiveness.
5. It offers a chance to restore the relationship.

Time passes too swiftly, and life is too short for arguments to linger, and every hour you spend angry is an hour you won't get back. Avoid the temptation to rehash old arguments. They make a horrible breakfast and a lousy mattress.

Be angry, but sin not. Don't let the sun go down while you are still mad. –Apostle Paul

7 GOOSE HER

Tickle Fight -- Some may think tickle fights are childish or silly, but nothing brings out giggles and laughter, like tickling your loved one with your fingertips, breath, a feather, flower, or lips. If you know ways to make your mate laugh, you also know the way to her heart.

You read that correctly –"Tickle Fight." Remember, we are still discussing what it takes to become a trophy husband. The idea is to encourage joy and laughter in your marriage. Laughter promotes relaxation and releases oxytocin, a hormone connected to well-being, empathy, trust, and closeness. In women and men, oxytocin increases during hugging and sex; thus, it is sometimes called the sex hormone.

Casually and lightly brushing your lover's skin can be electrifying and the perfect way of getting her attention. It may be the ticket to breaking the ice and leading to a time of intimacy.

Refrain from being so uptight that you are not having fun or taking time to play in your marriage. You must be a source of laughter and light-heartedness in your marriage and home. Your mate's laughter indicates she feels secure, content, and happy in your relationship and free to let her inhibitions go with you.

Sometimes in your relationship, nothing you do brings out her laughter. It may have nothing to do with what you did or failed to do. From time to time, we all occasionally need time to ourselves.

Should such a time come, don't try to force laughter or conversation out of her, and don't shut down because she is quiet. Be patient and considerate, and be available to her. Please don't stop talking because she is not talking. Try not to start a fight with her, and don't go out to the club or pub. Give her time!

8 HOLD HER HAND

Have you noticed your wife's reaction when she sees other men holding hands with their wives? If you hold her hand at the time, you will likely feel her squeeze yours. She does this because she feels honored and appreciated by you. She is grateful that you know how to value her.

Look at how others look at you when holding your wife's hand.

Holding hands is one of the simplest ways of adding to your relationship, and it's completely free. Reaching for your mate's hand when you walk through the park, pharmacy, or grocery store will demonstrate affection and comfort and cause her to feel more secure and vital. It will also remind her of better, simpler times in your relationship.

Holding hands with your mate will strengthen your bond, especially in stressful times. Stay close!

9 INTIMACY (IN-TO-ME-CEE)

Women need intimacy to love freely and without bounds in a loving relationship. You must periodically reassure her through commitment and loving gestures so she can feel entirely free to love you. Giving a woman flowers, expensive gifts, and warmed-over words after a tiff may not be enough. Work through problems calmly and quickly. Own up to mistakes fast. Be the man!

Men get excited by the sound of the female voice, the smell of her cologne, and the sight or feel of her skin, but our fairer female companions are far more complex. Your spouse needs more; you must woo her into feeling loving. Don't be alarmed by the terms "woo" and "complexity" -- her complexity is beautiful, which is why there are 26 ways to her heart.

Speaking calmly to your mate, holding her close, breathing with her, kissing, and touching are all forms of intimacy. Intimacy is the highest form of trust in a romantic relationship. Gentlemen, it will help to do these things long before you get to the bedroom.

10 JOKE WITH HER

We have discussed the importance of being amusing and knowing a few good jokes. Practice the art of being funny without being hurtful.

Jokes should never be personal, demeaning, or at your partner's expense. Honoring her means her secrets are safe with you, and her name is secure in your mouth. Never use her as the butt of your joke, and never" joke about her butt." Your presence and your arms are to your loved one's safe place. Laughing together keeps your love alive and keeps you both living longer.

Laughter - a merry heart does good like a medicine.
- King Solomon

11 KISS HER (ALL OVER)

This discussion aims to get you thinking about what's important to your mate and what makes her feel good in her relationship with you.

If you didn't know it already, you should know that kissing is one of your relationship's most intimate or sensual actions. It rates high on your mate's list of questions about you, and whether it seems juvenile or not, her girlfriends will or have already eventually asked, "Is he a good kisser?"

ALWAYS ensure your teeth, tongue, and breath are at their freshest level possible. Killerbreath will kill the moment. If you drink coffee and tea, use tobacco products, or enjoy the taste of onions, garlic, and spices, you must take extra precautions to ensure minty fresh breath.

Men don't spend much time thinking about kissing. However, you should remember that most women talk about kissing; if it is on her mind, it should also be yours.

Consider the following questions:

1. Do you remember your first kiss?
2. Did you practice beforehand?
3. How much do you know about kissing now?
4. Does your spouse enjoy your kisses?
5. How would you rate your kissing ability?
6. Are your kisses too sloppy or wet?
7. Are your kisses too dry?
8. Do your kisses last too long?

Which of the following kisses have you heard of or used? Which were most pleasurable or had the most effect on your partner?

1. Blowing kisses
2. Peck on the cheek
3. Forehead kisses
4. French kisses
5. Kiss on the hand
6. Stealing kisses
7. Closed-mouth kisses
8. Full- open-mouthed kiss
9. Nibbling
10. Eskimo kiss (Kunik) rubbing noses

Remember you are not bobbing for apples, deep-sea diving, or trying to resuscitate her. You are not trying to show how experienced you are at kissing or other acts. The idea is to express interest in your mate, not to get her to the bedroom. Demonstrating your experience level is not necessarily good; it could end your date prematurely.

Don't allow the hype about French kissing to excite you. Please don't make a big deal about it, especially on the first or early dates. What's appropriate? Is kissing necessary at all? Would a kiss on the hand or forehead suffice to signal your interest? Concentrate on making my date or your mate feel that she is important to you. Respect her, and respect yourself.

Should You Kiss Her?

Kissing, like any other form of intimacy, should not be something you do to fill a square. It's not like running the bases in baseball. It should not be something you fumble into, like players over a fumbled football.

A kiss, if appropriate, should be based on timing, i.e., if the moment is right and if that level of intimacy is something you both want. If you have no chemistry or compatibility, there should be no kissing.

If you are dating and have had an engaging conversation; your interests and goals are similar; smiles have been mutual, and there is apparent interest or chemistry between you, then a kiss may or may not be appropriate. Don't mess up a good thing by going too fast or too soon.

Be cautious, and be considerate -- try not to run in like an over-sexed boar in heat. Be considerate!

Where Kissing Leads

Kissing ignites passion and fuels desire. A kiss tells a partner you are interested in exploring a relationship beyond the date or taking your connection to the next level. For many, it means "hooking up" or bringing sex into the relationship. Be warned, at this point, that sex destroys many potentially good budding relationships.

This statement is not intended to be stuffy or outdated but a simple fact. Getting to know someone before becoming intimate is wise, as an aborted relationship is not the only danger. We have been duly warned about STDs and unwanted pregnancies. Contrary to popular opinion, condoms and contraceptives are less reliable than depicted. Whatever you do on your date or outing, exercise self-control.

12 LEAD, LISTEN, LOVE

No husband's role is as critical or misunderstood as his home leadership role. What often complicates this is an old mindset that demands ultimate authority and the last word. The truth is, anytime one has to say they are in charge, it indicates that they are not in control. I hate to burst anyone's bubble, but authentic leadership is not vested in us as males just because we have a penis. When you are leading, you'll never have to say it.

When we consider that millions of women manage thriving, healthy households without a man at the helm, it shoots a broad hole in the argument or presumption that we must be in charge.

The most effective leadership in married households is a partnership, not a dictatorship. When a husband views his wife as an equal partner, there will rarely be an instance where who is in charge becomes an issue or argument. In partnerships, strengths and abilities may differ, but you remain equals. We must remember we are both on the same team.

A husband who recognizes and appreciates his mate's strengths will not permit his ego to get in the way of progress. His family will love and honor him, and his children will be better prepared for life and marriage because they have a positive example of a father and husband.

13 MASTER MASSAGES

Ironically, an unmarried Apostle Paul taught, **"Men ought to love their wives as they do their "own" bodies, which they nourish and cherish."**

He added, **"Men are to serve their wives as Christ did the church, by giving Himself for it."** Essentially, we are to promote the absolute best for our mates through our example.

In this light, we are to observe our wives. You need to demonstrate concern if she is in pain or discomfort in any area. Determine the source, level, and kind of pain.

A word here for new and potential husbands, at some point in your marriage, you may need to go to the pharmacy to pick up feminine products, test kits, and like items. No need to complain or be embarrassed; we have been there too. Remember, she might need to pick up some personal products for you someday.

Foot, back, and shoulder rubs and deep-tissue massages are miracle cures and a sure way of gaining her trust and attention. If she does not need a doctor, grab a towel, bath oils, lotions, and scented candles, and go to work.

She will wonder what you are doing if you have given her a massage before. Be patient and talk her through your process. Tell her you are reading about "Becoming a Trophy Husband" and need practice.

Roll up your sleeves and go to work. As you do this, you're both going to learn a lot.

Don't stress — take it slow, and be gentle unless she wants a firmer touch. Concentrate on working out her kinks from head to toe. Be patient; even if she goes to sleep, you are doing good work, and it will pay off - big!

If you need more information on planning for administering a massage, grab a copy of our book, "Erogenous Zones - Exploring Marital Intimacy." Get your copy at https://bit.ly/getyourezoness or http://bit.ly/intimatezone

14 NAKED AND UNASHAMED

The Bible states, *"Adam and Eve were in the garden, and they were naked and unashamed." (Genesis 2:25)*

I am not trying to make an intellectual or religious argument here. I want to point out a few things about Adam and Eve's living arrangement that should benefit us.

a. God created Adam, and He later created Eve so Adam would have companionship.

b. The two were naked until they ate the forbidden fruit, then realized they were naked.

c. They lived in a beautiful Garden, which means everything else they did was outside.

d. They made a choice that got them kicked out of the garden.

e. God wants us to be happy in marriage.

f. God wants us to enjoy each other.

g. There should be no shame in marital intimacy.

h. We should not feel inhibited in expressing love when we obey God's law.

i. We are at our best when satisfied sexually in the confines of marriage.

j. Finally, we experience difficulties whenever we deviate from God's plan.

What God wants for your marriage:

a. Your happiness.
b. Communicate freely and effectively.
c. Uninhibited in expressing love for each other.
d. Complete sexual satisfaction in your marriage
e. Ultimate intimacy in your marriage.
f. Free from shame, embarrassment, and guilt.
g. Secrets shared between you will remain secret.

15 OPEN UP

You may have noticed that your wife tends to get frustrated that you are not as open with her as she would like. Most of us males are in the same club. We are uncomfortable expressing emotions or saying how we feel. While women regularly share, we tend to be more tight-lipped. What does she want?

Your wife is not expecting you to be her. She wants to know that you are alive, that you love her, and that you are interested in what she thinks and feels. You will be happy that you try to tell her what is on your mind. Her frustration will not likely go away quickly, but some tools can help you become more available if you are willing to use them.

Think about how many people whose marriages have reached a dead-end because they lack the will or ability to solve their problems. I understand some things won't come easy, but just as you do the homework to figure out why your kitchen lights are flickering, you must use the same effort and commitment to communicate with your mate.

I cannot promise these tools will work if you need help with an abusive or violent temperament, substance abuse, infidelity, sexual perversion, or refusal to work. I would love to help you get help with those issues. Reach out to us at marriagemakes3.com

If communication is lacking in your marriage, try setting aside 30 minutes every few days to talk. Just say, "Honey, I love you, and what you have to say is important to me. I want us to have some uninterrupted time to talk. "Can we set aside 30 minutes every day or two to hang out?" She will be more open to spending time with you if you ask her while helping to wash dishes or if you volunteer to take over other housework.

For many men, taking on new or unconventional chores might require a change in mindset. Remember that all you do is for the common good. You are on the same team.

Truthfully, many women also work outside the home and often do an unfair share of housework. They drop off and pick up children from school, ballet, choir, and band rehearsals; in addition to the housework, and laundry, they prepare meals, get children ready for bed, then start over the following day.

She may not feel she has fifteen minutes to spare. Your job is to ensure you take enough off her plate so that she can give you the 30 minutes you requested.

Great relationships require sacrifice, which may mean you must watch a prerecorded game or match instead of seeing it at a friend's man cave or club sports bar to give her more time for you

Your Homework

Before the designated time you both set aside, jot down three to four questions and discussion topics for when you are alone with your spouse.

When you get that time alone, eliminate all distractions. Practice listening and responding to demonstrate your interest in your mate's concerns.

Initially, your actions might seem robotic or less than sincere. But don't despair; you will improve as you practice this technique. Your questions and conversation will become more spontaneous and natural.

Even if your spouse has nothing more to say during your time together, commit to regularly being in each other's presence. Opening up to your spouse in conversation will eliminate communication barriers and bring you closer in other areas of your relationship. Gradually she will start to want this time alone to get some of her words out, and the time will become more relaxed.

Have you ever noticed how easy it is to communicate when we want something? That's it – You want something from her. **Speaking of "Something** we want," -- wives also need their husbands to be more open and expressive sexually.

Invest in Knowing

Don't assume you know everything about your wife sexually or in any other respect. Women have a wonderful element of mystery that evades us. We all have that capacity for growth. Our wives are still evolving and want us to understand what they need and for us to communicate what we need.

Most men want quantity (or we think we do), while women want quality and variety. Quality and variety have to do with creative approaches and a change of scenery and location. Women equate quality with forethought and preparation.

She will adore you for reading to her from her favorite novel, or The Songs of Solomon, while she drives or relaxes. If you have difficulty reading, get an audio version of the books or Bible, and listen to it with her. Whether she is driving or not, she will be relaxed and appreciative by the end of your trip. We build good relationships through sacrifices and acts of kindness. Your putting in the extra effort will pay big dividends for your marriage.

Let me pose a couple of questions:

1. Are there rooms in your home besides your bedroom?

2. Do you own a truck, van, or car?

3. Is there a garage or storage building on your property?

4. Do you have a fenced backyard?

5. Is there a barn or work shed if you live on a farm?

Are you following me so far? Use your imagination to fully take advantage of these features of your home or property.

Here is a question for those who may be a little uneasy about sexual matters – Where were Adam and Eve's children conceived?

If your answer included "Garden" or "outside," you are starting to understand. While the outside might not be best for you and yours, the point is if you are limiting time alone with your spouse to your bedroom and only at night, you are cheating yourself and your mate. What I am saying is, "Be creative. Think outside the bedroom."

You should not think your mate a freak or end up wanting more creativity and variety from sex. I suggest that by giving your mate what she wants, you will get what you want and more. Opening up is effectively communicating your desires and learning what your mate likes. Be willing to learn and try something new. The end goal is always your mutual satisfaction and growing in your love for each other. Your passion thrives; you establish trust by meeting her needs and protecting her sensibilities.

I indicated before that "We men THINK we want quantity." WORK to get the QUALITY and VARIETY she wants and your relationship deserve. In focusing on those three, you'll realize YOU & YOUR bride are getting what you wanted.

17 PRIEST, PROVIDER, PROTECTOR, PRESENCE

Each husband should strive for four crucial roles in marriage and home; everything else falls in line when we do so. These roles are priest, protector, provider, and presence. He should strive to make sure all the bases are covered. I don't mean a husband should try to do all this just because he is the husband. The wife may be better at some things. It makes little sense for me to struggle with family finances when my wife is an accountant.

PRIESTS – As priests in the home, husbands, and fathers are to be the closest representation of God in the home. He is to help bring the household into a relationship with God by praying for and leading the family to a relationship with God. The Bible patriarch Job is a sterling example of a husband who carried out his priestly responsibilities well. He prayed for his children and made offerings to God on their behalf. The community honored Job and called him whenever they needed divine counsel.

Sadly, it is in priestly duties that men fail most often. Men in most households are content to let their mates lead the family in worship and religious obligations. We have as much responsibility to lead in religion as we do in providing for and protecting our families. And we have more to lose since God gave us this responsibility. I'm not suggesting women should not fulfill the role; I'm saying she should not do it alone.

PROVIDERS meet the family's daily needs: food, clothing, shelter, safety, and medical necessity. Although these are the most basic needs, transportation and education are necessities. Although you may view these responsibilities as yours as a husband, it is unwise to ignore the contributions of a loving wife, whether she works in or outside the home.

As **PROTECTORS**, husbands should be the first line of defense for the home, putting themselves in any danger the household may face. To protect means taking steps to secure the home and family — physically, financially, or in any other way necessary. Installing a home security and camera system, repairing doors, windows, and locks, and securing home and life insurance policies are actions taken to help safeguard the family. Most men are hardwired to provide for and protect the family and will do so to their harm. We can see tangible results in providing and protecting. We understand that we minimize worry for our mates in fulfilling these roles.

PRESENCE- (being present – at home). In the United States, men are primarily valued based on what they provide. They tend to feel that their work is done as long as the family has shelter, food, and clothing and is financially and physically secure. Many men have sacrificed their presence, i.e., time with the family for long work hours, leaving wives and moms to carry a bigger load in maintaining the home and raising children.

18 QUESTIONS?

Fellows, if you know anything about women, they are not afraid to ask questions. They will ask if you are okay if you are too quiet. Her questions will likely be more persistent if you are evasive; tell her half the story or give her misleading information.

Men must remember that women are incubators. "Give her flowers, and she will make a garden. Give her seed, and she will give you a baby; Give her a house, and she will make a home; Give her crap, and.... Let's say, You might not like the taste of your sandwich.

Practice being open, honest, and accountable, just as you want her to be to you. If you have ever been unfaithful or less than truthful with her, your transparency, honesty, and faithfulness are even more critical.

Over the years, many marriages settle into routines and ruts, and needs remain unspoken and unfulfilled. Far too many couples wake up one day and realize they have grown apart and no longer have the same or shared interests. They are no longer as close as they once were. Can it be that they never knew each other? Can it be that they are not listening or communicating?

Men, trust me when I tell you, she IS listening to you. She can probably tell you how often you ask her where your keys are and how many times a month you lose your keys. Yes, Guys we are more predictable and easy to read. She can tell when your answers are less than sincere or truthful. Are you listening as intently to her?

Are You listening to her?

1. What is your wife's birthday?
2. What is her favorite color?
3. Does she like flowers, and what is her favorite?
4. Does she like receiving gifts or spending time with you?
5. Does she like essential oils and perfumes?
6. What is her favorite scent?
7. Would your wife prefer that you build or buy her something?
8. Does she enjoy surprises?
9. Would your mate prefer a gift or that you take her somewhere?

Congratulations if you know all the answers. You are an exception. Only some men get all the answers right. It is likely that by the time you learn the answers, one of them will change. Men generally marry, hoping their wives never change, and women marry men, hoping they will cooperate with the process. Try to keep up. She likes pink today; you may be surprised in a few years to learn that she likes brown. Try not to sweat it; we are all trying to keep up.

A-S-K

You keep up with your mate by ASKING QUESTIONS & LISTENING TO HER ANSWERS. Good questions are the foundation for good conversation; both are critical for good communication and thriving relationships. Talking together will draw you together and keep you together.

> Heaven has no rage like love to hatred turned, nor Hell a fury like a woman scorned.
>
> – William Congreve

19 ROMANCE HER

Overall, women delight in the courtesies extended by the man who loves and adores them. They love the excitement and mystery associated with love. Since some women reject such courtesies as sexist, some men have trouble keeping up with what is acceptable. – Some men have stopped being mysterious, exciting, and romantic.

Although what constitutes romance differs with each person, most women generally like having the door opened for them and appreciate their partner pulling out their chair or helping with their coat.

If you have trouble keeping up, romance is merely loving gestures extended to one's romantic partner or lover. Examples include embracing, kissing, holding hands, whispering sweet nothings, low light, soft music, champagne toasts, being close to each other, surprises, speaking to each other's hearts, and reassuring each other of your love. Each couple must decide what is appropriate for them in romance.

What you should know about being romantic is that it strengthens your marriage bond. It is a long-term investment in your wife's self-esteem. It is an investment in how she will remember you in the future.

Witnessing your romance with your wife will also positively affect your children and grandchildren. They will remember how you loved their mother or grandmother.

Being romantic is a positive example for your son to emulate. Your daughter will look for a husband based on the kind of husband you are to her mother. Do your best to be a good example rather than a horrible warning.

In romancing your wife, we recommend you plan for special treatment, whether dating at home or going out elsewhere. Put in a lot of effort to make the occasion special. Do not wait for special occasions to be romantic.

Occasionally, plan to date at home. Clean up and dress up, find out what she likes, then do it, and add a few surprises of your choosing.

20 SAY IT

Saying "I LOVE YOU" is not just something you only say on special occasions. It is best when you express it daily with words and actions.

A woman once complained that her husband "Never tells me that he loves me." When asked what he says when she tells him, she replies, "He says, "Okay" or "Thank you."

When asked why he never tells her he loves her, he said," I told her when we married in 1962, and nothing changed. I am still here."

Unlike women, some men can live without hearing "I love you."Men must demonstrate sacrificial love daily, putting their mates' needs first. Secondly, men must learn to love their mates the way their mate wants to be loved. Fathers who show affectionate love to their wives are the best examples of how to love and value their mates. Children who live with affection are likelier to have successful relationships when they become adults.

21 TAME THAT MANE!

I am sure there was a collective "Moan" as various men read this topic. I am unsure what it is about parents' reluctance to give their son his first haircut and the adult male's hesitation in cutting away undergrowth from "down south" and our backsides.

People whose poor babies resembled werewolf cubs say things like, "It's bad luck if boys get their first haircut before they are a year old," and "If he gets his hair cut this soon, he won't be as strong."

Some of you are thinking about it; let's say it together -- "Double Poppycock!"

In recent years, full beards have become high fashion. When nicely maintained, they are great. But, if you are sporting three years' growth, have never trimmed, and seldom washed, then you are overdue for a complete shave and a wash. If your beard has crumbs from last week's meals, or if hairs from your mustache, nose, ears, eyebrows, and head have formed a conglomerate, "You need to cut it."

I fear "beards gone wild" is just the tip of the iceberg. In a recent survey, women listed untrimmed back and butt hair as the top turn-offs for sexual intimacy with their mates. In a similar poll, women listed men's testicles as the least desirable place for uncontrolled hair growth.

Talk to your doctor and barber about solutions for uncontrolled hair growth. A local SPA or beauty supply will also have suggestions. Many hair removal products are also available in your local and online stores.

One cannot help but wonder if superstitions about cutting hair are why some men allow a virtual wasteland to develop below. No evidence supports that trimming the hair down south will affect your potency or virility.

However, you should know that excessive and unwashed hair in the pubic area can potentially limit your pleasure by creating a haven for bacteria and off-putting odors.

If your partner tends to avoid your southern region, that is a good hint that things could be better. If you are still in doubt, her avoiding you indicates that you have work to do in the maintenance department.

Begin by safely trimming away excess growth—pubic hair length averages from 0.5 to 1.5 inches and longer in some people. If hair exceeds one-half inch, I suggest a trim.

Ensure you are regularly washing with antibacterial soap, then deodorizing. Many natural soaps and deodorants are available, so there is no reason to offend yourself or others.

Let's face it; we occasionally let ourselves go. Long winter months, coronavirus, social distancing, and isolation might have all contributed to why we have let things go too far.

Ultimately, it is up to you to maintain your face and body. But you must realize that what one person considers sexy is another person's turn-off. When it comes to getting close, remember that smooth and good smelling works most of the time; rough occasionally works, but smelly never works. You must know what your partner prefers.

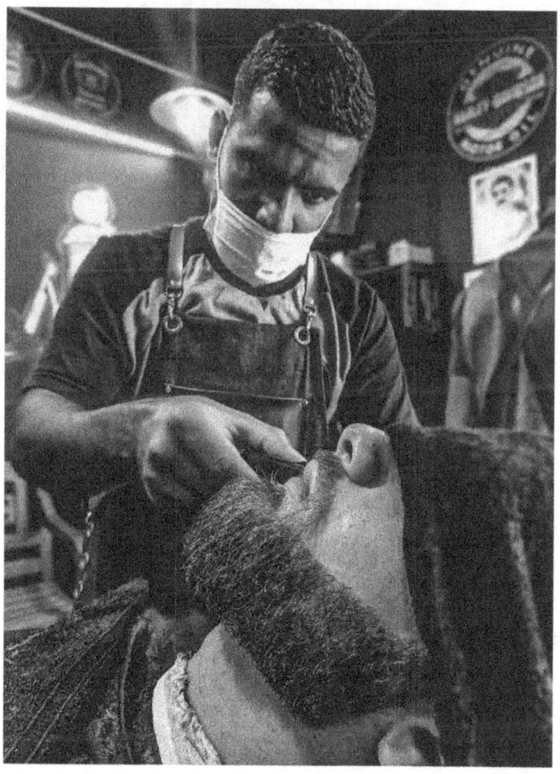

22 UNISEX

I am sure the topic caught your eye. Unisex has to do with fashions and hairstyles believed to be suitable for either sex. I want to talk about some jobs around the home that either of you may do. Most men acknowledge and readily accept responsibility for making a living and providing for their families. We embrace responsibility for home maintenance, yard work, and other so-called manly chores. But we don't always share in the household chores or caring for our children. How many have told others, "I'm busy babysitting?" When they are our children, we should say, "I'm busy parenting."

The point is that sometimes, it's the language we use that keeps us from trophy status.

Being unable to cook should not be an excuse for men or women with spouses and children. You can learn. Men, your stock values will soar if you master a few dishes. Your woman will think highly of you when you give her an occasional break without her asking. You can still work the grill if she tells you to stay out of my kitchen. –No excuses.

Some issues with men's household roles stem from changes within the last 30 years. We must understand that more and more women have pursued education and a career and may now work outside the home. Like their male counterparts and companions, they bring home a paycheck. Yet, they are still often expected to handle most household responsibilities.

Guys, even if you initially suck at household chores, your spouse will be thrilled you are doing the work. Keep at it, and you will improve.

Nothing strengthens a marriage like the two of you working side-by-side. Remember, marriage is spelled "W-O-R-K." It's suitable for everyone.

23 VALUE HER

Everyone wants to be valued and appreciated in life, especially in love.

Come to think of it, isn't that what we do with our trophies? We put them in a lighted display case where we view them as a reminder of our accomplishments. We give them a place of prominence in our homes, where they can be seen and appreciated.

A big part of valuing your spouse is to involve her in the decision process. With most essential decisions, there will be adequate time to discuss things. Should you ever have to make a solo decision, you should know her well enough to know how she might feel. Use your best judgment and bring her in on it right away.

Men, never leave your spouse with any doubt as to how you feel about her. Love her, listen to her; speak gently to her; honor her above all else. Be the man you want your son to become and the kind of man you want your daughter to marry. Hold your bride in the highest esteem, and she will do the same.

Another way of valuing a spouse is by keeping her from being overburdened at home. Her biggest task is managing children's meals, clothing, assignments, extracurricular activities, and bedtimes. You can substantially change the hurried dynamics of your home by taking on the part of this cumbersome duty. Plan your evening by checking in with your spouse. Is there anything special you need to know? If so, use this as the starting point.

If not, prioritize spending time with each child according to their needs. Ask open-ended questions about their day. At first, keep the topics light before moving on to issues like schoolwork, friendships, and problem areas.

At first, your children may resist your intrusion if you haven't spent much time with them. Gradually, they will become accustomed and may even look forward to their time with you. Don't wholly exclude mom since she has been doing this without you. Bring her in with challenging issues and when a child may play one parent against the other.

Concentrate on teaching your children to solve school and life problems. Don't hesitate to intervene when their safety and well-being are issues. Also, make sure you are involved in PTA or PTO meetings. to ensure consistency between what your child tells you and what their teacher tells you. Check-in with mom to ensure she is okay with the arrangement. You might want to switch roles periodically.

24 W-O-R-D-S

I am sure you have heard it — women talk more than men. Women use an average of 20,000 words daily, while men average less than 1/3 of that, at approximately 7,000 words daily. Thus, it seems well-founded when women complain that their men do not talk enough.

Guys, if we are not talking, we may not be listening, responding, or following up on what women are saying to us.

Given this dynamic, we can understand why most relationships end primarily from poor communication.

Consider these six tips for changing your communication game:

1. Listen intently and without distractions.

2. Put away cell phones and other devices.

3. Show that you are listening by responding in kind. Respond with words, questions, and feelings.

4. Ask questions for clarity and interest, and ensure you can follow the conversation.

5. If she typically likes to talk when you get home, ask for time to shower or freshen up to be better equipped to listen.

6. Choose a secluded place, away from playing children, television noise, and other distractions.

Look at her when she is talking. Your eye contact and verbal interaction prove to her that you are fully engaged in the conversation.

When the conversation ends, don't run off. Briefly clarify what was said. Summarize the discussion and address any questions you may have.

Conclude your time together by engaging further. Taking your mate's hand, reminding her that you love and appreciate her. Hold her close for a few minutes, especially if the conversation concerns something you did or failed to do. I know this part can be frustrating; we've all been there. When necessary, swallow your pride, and apologize. I can promise you are going to get good results. I can promise you are going to get good results. You never can tell where it all might lead.

25 EXPRESS YOURSELF

If we have talked much about communication, you are starting to grasp how important it is in your relationships. If you are also a parent, try to remember that you are also modeling the proper behavior for your son or daughter.

Forty-eight percent of first marriages end in divorce. Seventy-eight percent of second marriages fail. Primary reasons include infidelity, lack of commitment, money worries, debt, and abuse. The common factor in every divorce is that they can no longer communicate.

Consider these benefits and steps in daily conversations with your partner:

. 1. Remember that conversation connects you.

. 2. Be vulnerable; speak softly.

. 3. Quickly admit when you are wrong.

. 4. Own up to your mistakes quickly.

. 5. Never strike or abuse your spouse in any manner.

. 6. Everyday conversations bring you closer in all areas of your relationship.

. 7. Opening to your spouse exposes your heart to intimacy.

. 8. Everyday conversations bring you closer to other areas.

26 YOUR MODEL MAY DIFFER

While most women have similar basic needs, your wife will have remarkable differences in keeping with her unique personality, experience, and preferences. These are differences that make her, unlike any other woman. You will be wise to identify, love, and appreciate the differences.

For example, some women do not care for flowers, chocolates, or wine. Others are not big on receiving gifts but may prefer to spend time or ride with you. She might appreciate your words of affirmation more than expensive gifts, trips, and the like.

The key to a great marriage is getting to know and appreciate her for who she is. Understand that she is evolving, and the person she is now will gradually change. Do not let this scare you; it is healthy, growing people do. Observe, study, and love the person she is, and do not miss the subtle change. Think about ways your mate has changed since you first met.

Many men tend to change when something forces them to do so. Let's test this theory –

Do you have a pair of undies that have several holes in them? What motivated your last underwear purchase?

Many of you will say your wife bought them for you or told you to remove the old ones.

Here is another example -

Have you ever started a long overdue home project because your wife started to do it herself or called a repair person to complete it?

Apostle Peter, who was himself married, wrote: **Husbands, dwell with your wives according to knowledge, honoring your wife, as unto the weaker vessel, and as heirs together of the grace of life; so that your prayers are not hindered. (1 Peter 3:7)**

The phrase, *according to knowledge,* implies that men must study their wives just as one prepares to master a subject or obtain a degree or promotion. As healthy people, you and your mate will continue to grow over the years. So, it would help if you committed to a lifetime of study to keep up with each other. Your mate is unlike anyone else in the world. She may not be as expressive or emotional or ask as many questions as others. Avoid comparing her to others.

In studying your mate, you will know your mate's needs, moods, weaknesses, and strengths. Remember, we also have needs, attitudes, liabilities, and abilities. Exercise the same patience with her you would like her to show you.

27 ZERBERTS

"What is a Zerbert?" – you ask. Let's try a little demonstration:

1. Hold up your left hand.

2. Turn the back of your hand slightly toward your face.

3. Lift your hand to your mouth.

4. Moisten your lips slightly.

5. Place your lips over the meaty part of your hand.

6. Adjust your lips so air can escape from the corner of your mouth.

7. Inhale, pucker up, and blow onto the fleshy part of your hand.

Hear the comical sound of air escaping? That was a "Zerbert." Congratulations! To experience the power of Zerberts, practice them with your bride.

Exercise caution, and use Zerberts sparingly, as they may annoy your mate if used indiscriminately or overused. Zerberts like tickling can trigger leakage.

Ensure your partner has an opportunity to the bathroom before administering them. Otherwise, they may produce the same effects as tickling, such as laughter, playfulness, and sexual desire.

Experiment with these application sites:

1. Your mate's inner wrist
2. Bend of the elbow
3. Back of the knees
4. Sides and back of the neck
5. Shoulder blades
6. Sides
7. Inner thighs

Zerberts can be applied anywhere the body has a valley, low place, or padded area. Your imagination and your spouse's sensitivities and cooperation are only the determining factors. Make **Zerberts** part of your fun, foreplay, kissing, massage, and the other things we have mentioned. Some of you will remember how you practiced kissing. Here is where you put all the skills together.

I have included this section to remind you to do fun stuff. If you winced or frowned every time you saw the word, you may have forgotten to have fun or have become so busy that you are no longer as open to having fun together.

28 BENEFITS OF BECOMING

A TROPHY HUSBAND

1. You will have a greater sense of accountability.

2. There will be fewer disagreements between you.

3. You will be more considerate of your mate's needs.

4. There will be greater intimacy between you.

5. You will have improved communication between you.

6. Your mate will have a greater appreciation for you.

7. She will agree with more of your choices.

8. She will speak well of you.

9. She will have fewer questions about where you go

10. There will be improved mutual respect between you.

11. The honor between you will multiply.

12. You will continue to grow as an individual.

13. You will grow together

14. You will spend less time in the doghouse.

15. You will have a good marriage.

16. You will enjoy less stress & better health.

17. You will have more productivity; improved workflow.

18. You will enjoy better financial stability.

19. Your children will be more secure in who they are.

20. Your children will have a surer future.

21. Your children will have more respect for you both.

22. Your marriage will honor God.

23. You will laugh more.

24. You will love more.

25. You will live longer.

29 CONCLUSION

I set out to write the book I wish was available as a young man, which I could feel good about putting into the hands of sons like mine. I wrote it hoping to keep others from learning lessons I learned the hard way.

God has graciously taught me; I'm better off for what I endured and learned.

I have been privileged to marry a trophy wife and have lived blissfully with her for 16 years. I owe this book in part to her. She has suggested for the last six or seven years that I should be teaching "Husband Classes." So, here are the first 26 lessons.

I use these tools daily in my marriage, and they will work for you. I cannot promise a miracle, but anything is possible when you are willing to try and trust God.

There is hope for you if you struggle with your temper, abuse, anger, and self-control issues. Seek help. These issues will keep you from enjoying a lifetime of love. God has better in mind for you, but you must ask for it.

ABOUT THE AUTHOR

GREGORY D MOSTELLA, DMIN

The author is a retired United States Air Force Veteran. He has pastored for over 40 years in Guam, Japan, North Dakota, Alabama, and Mississippi. He is the author of six books, including So You Think You're Called to Ministry, a two-book series, Crushed: Finding Meaning in Suffering, Breaking Nets and Sinking Ships, and Erogenous Zones - Discovering Marital Intimacy, which he co-authored with Dr. Michelle Sandy Mostella, his bride of almost 16 years.

Drs. Gregory and Michelle founded Marriage and Family R-US, a nonprofit seeking to rescue under-served and at-risk families by helping couples achieve marriage success through specialized training and counseling programs.

Look for their content on @marriageandfamilyrus on Instagram, Facebook, and Twitter and www.marriagemakes3.com and www.marriageandfamilyrus.org

Relationship Counselors

"MY LORD, MY LOVER AND ME"

Doctors Gregory Dale & Michelle Sandy Mostella

Our mission, as spiritual relationship counselors, instructors, and mentors is to get you unstuck and moving forward in your relationship. Whether you are married, single, or in between, we use Biblical principles to get you on track by listening to you, then giving you the tools to get you going. We remain in your corner throughout the process, guiding, inspiring, and praying for you.

If you are single and want to be married, we help you identify why matrimony has eluded you, and we give you the tools to help get you ready for "I do."

If your marriage is in troubled waters, we identify solutions and guide you to improved communication, finances, intimacy, family dynamics, and working together so that your marriage lasts.

If you are considering or recovering from divorce, we give you the tools to help you work together to get past affairs, entanglements, and past difficulties restored to wholeness. Whether you remain married or go through with the divorce, you still need to be healed and whole

marriageandfamilyrus.org

The e-Book AVAILABLE NOW on AMAZON

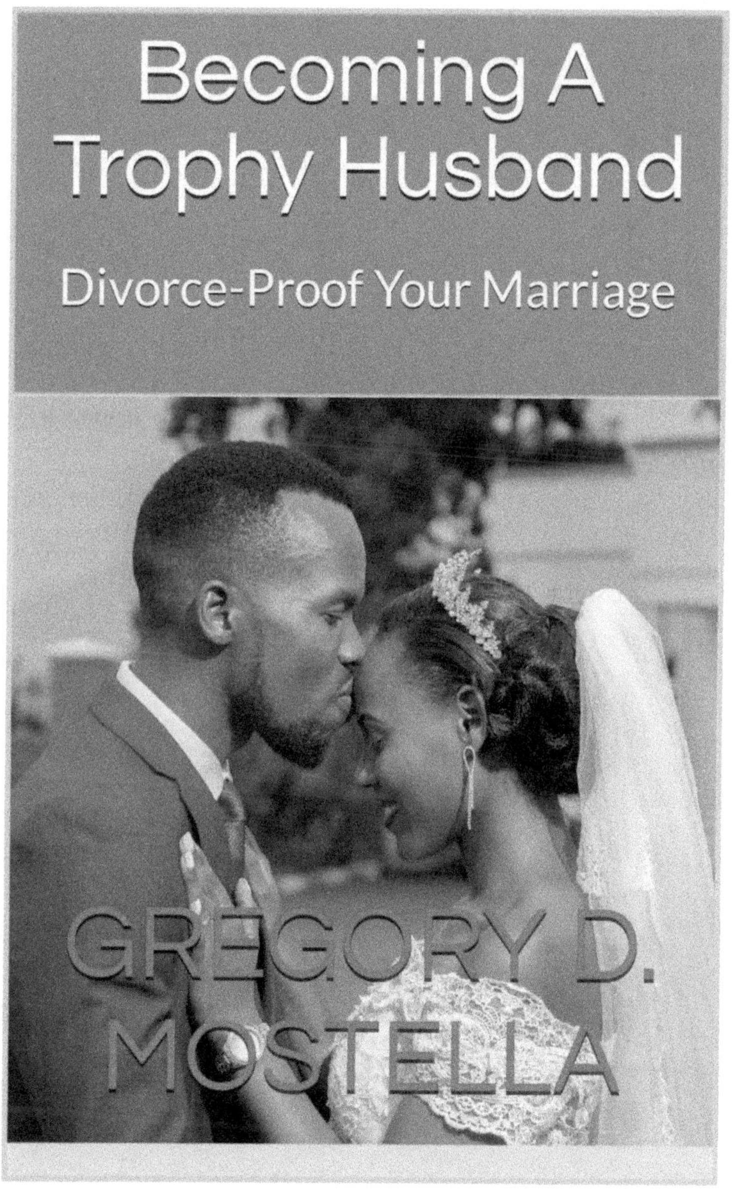